# Laughing Time

## COLLECTED NONSENSE

# LAUGHING TIME

## COLLECTED NONSENSE

## WILLIAM JAY SMITH

### PICTURES BY
### FERNANDO KRAHN

FARRAR STRAUS GIROUX • NEW YORK

Some of the poems in this collection first appeared
in the following books by William Jay Smith:
*Laughing Time, Boy Blue's Book of Beasts,*
*Puptents and Pebbles, Mr. Smith and Other Nonsense,*
*Typewriter Town,* and *The New York Kids' Book,*
and also in *Cricket* magazine and *The New York Times.*

Library of Congress catalog card number: 90-55655
Published simultaneously in Canada by
HarperCollins*CanadaLtd*
Printed in the United States of America
First edition, 1980
Revised edition, 1990

To
Marissa and Alexandre

# CONTENTS

**The King of Hearts**                    *3*

LAUGHING TIME                             *5*
Laughing Time                             *7*
Why                                       *8*
The Land of Ho-Ho-Hum                     *9*
Around My Room                           *10*
Hats                                     *10*
Jack-in-the-Box                         *11*
Over and Under                          *12*
Apples                                   *13*
The Mirror                               *13*
Spilt Milk: Whodunit                    *14*
Up the Hill                             *16*
The Toaster                             *17*
Moon                                    *18*
Mrs. Caribou                            *20*
Alice                                   *22*
Dictionary                              *23*
When Candy Was Chocolate                *24*
Big and Little                          *25*
Jittery Jim                             *27*
Molly Mock-Turtle                       *28*
Love                                    *28*
My Body                                 *29*

The Panda                       30
Grandmother Ostrich             30
Pick Me Up                      31
The Queen of the Nile           32
Fish                            33
Mistress Mary                   34
People                          35
Having                          36
Betsy Robin                     37
The Owl                         37
Things                          38

PUPTENTS AND PEBBLES:
A Nonsense ABC                  41

BOY BLUE'S BEASTS               57
Elephant                        58
Monkey                          59
Tiger                           60
Yak                             61
Parrot (from Trinidad)          62
Antelope                        63
Pig                             64
Lion                            65
Camel                           66
Seal                            67
Dragon                          68
Whale                           70
Opossum                         71
Unicorn                         72
Kangaroo                        73
Hen                             74
Anteater                        75

Mole                                          76
Rhinoceros                                    77
Coati-Mundi                                   78
Zebra                                         79
Water Buffalo                                 79
Gooney Bird                                   80
Butterfly                                     81
Crocodile                                     82
Tapir                                         84
Hippopotamus                                  85
Cat                                           86
Dog                                           87
Fox and Crow                                  88
Cow                                           89
Parrot (from Zambezi)                         90
Gull                                          91
Raccoon                                       92
Penguin                                       94
Polar Bear                                    94
Giraffe                                       95
Swan                                          96


THE OLD MAN FROM OKEFENOKEE:
Loony and Lopsided Limericks                  97


BROOKLYN BRIDGE                              109
A Visit to the Mayor                         110
Brooklyn Bridge                              112
Subway Centipede                             114
King Kong Bat                                115
The Easter Parade                            116
Bay-Breasted Barge Bird                      117
The Grease Monkey and the Powder Puff        118

IMAGINARY DIALOGUES                        119

A CLUTCH OF CLERIHEWS                      123

A NUTHATCH OF NONSENSE BIRDS              127
Chit-Chat                                  128
Faucet                                     128
Collector Bird                             128
Cat-Whiskered Catbird                      129
Hackle Bird                                129
Pigeon-toed Pigeons                        130
Hoolie Bird                                130
Slant-eyed Peeker                          130
Dollar Bird                                131
Upside-Down Bird                           131
Common Mudlatch                            131
Postman Pelican                            132
Gondola Swan                               133
Executive Eagle                            133
Television Toucan                          134
Horn-rimmed Hen                            134
Rage                                       134
Dressmaking Screamer                       135
Zipper Bird                                135
Walking-Stick Bird                         136

NONSENSE COOKERY                           139
Canapés *à la Poste*                       140
Hot and Cold Tin-Can Surprise             140
Chocolate Moose                            141

THE FLOOR AND THE CEILING                  143
The Floor and the Ceiling                  144

Little Dimity                              146
Big Gumbo                                 147
Banjo Tune                                148
The Crossing of Mary of Scotland          149
The Black Widow                           150
Bad Boy's Swan Song                       151
The Antimacassar and the Ottoman          152
Flight of the One-eyed Bat                154
Flight of the Long-haired Yak             156
Ballad of Black and White                 158
May-as-Well                               160
The Typewriter Bird                       161
Mr. Smith                                 162

**The King of Spain**                     164

# LAUGHING TIME

## COLLECTED NONSENSE

# THE KING OF HEARTS

*"I like this book," said the King of Hearts.*
*"It makes me laugh the way it starts!"*

*"I like it also!" said his Mother.*
*So they sat down and read it to each other.*

# LAUGHING
# TIME

# LAUGHING TIME

It was laughing time, and the tall Giraffe
Lifted his head, and began to laugh:

Ha! Ha!   Ha! Ha!

And the Chimpanzee on the ginkgo tree
Swung merrily down with a *Tee Hee Hee:*

Hee! Hee!   Hee! Hee!

"It's certainly not against the law!"
Croaked Justice Crow with a loud guffaw:

Haw! Haw!   Haw! Haw!

The dancing Bear who could never say "No"
Waltzed up and down on the tip of his toe:

Ho! Ho!   Ho! Ho!

The Donkey daintily took his paw,
And around they went: Hee-Haw! Hee-Haw!

Hee-Haw!   Hee-Haw!

The Moon had to smile as it started to climb;
All over the world it was laughing time!

Ho! Ho!   Ho! Ho!   Hee-Haw!   Hee-Haw!
Hee! Hee!   Hee! Hee!   Ha! Ha!   Ha! Ha!

# WHY

Why do apricots look like eggs?
       Why?
Why do sofas have four legs?
       Why?
Why do buses stop and go?
Why do roosters strut and crow?
Why do bugles blow and blow?
Why is Sunday? I don't know
       Why!

# THE LAND OF
# HO·HO·HUM

When you want to go wherever you please,
Just sit down in an old valise,
    And fasten the strap
    Around your lap,
And fly off over the apple trees.

And fly for days and days and days
Over rivers, brooks, and bays
    Until you come
    To Ho-Ho-Hum,
Where the Lion roars, and the Donkey brays.

Where the Unicorn's tied to a golden chain,
And Umbrella Flowers drink the rain.
    After that,
    Put on your hat,
Then sit down and fly home again.

# AROUND MY ROOM

I put on a pair of overshoes
And walk around my room,
With my Father's bamboo walking stick,
And my Mother's feather broom.

I walk and walk and walk and walk,
I walk and walk around.
I love my Father's tap-tap-tap,
My Mother's feathery sound.

# HATS

Round or square
Or tall or flat,
People love
To wear a hat.

# JACK-IN-THE-BOX

A Jack-in-the-Box
On the pantry shelf
Fell in the coffee
And hurt himself.
Nobody looked
To see what had happened:
There by the steaming
Hot urn he lay;
So they picked him up
With the silverware
And carried him off
On the breakfast tray.

# OVER AND UNDER

Bridges are for going over water,
Boats are for going over sea;
Dots are for going over dotted *i*'s,
And blankets are for going over me.

Over and under,
  Over and under,
    Crack the whip,
      And hear the thunder.

Divers are for going under water,
Seals are for going under sea;
Fish are for going under mermaids' eyes,
And pillows are for going under me.

Over and under,
  Over and under,
    Crack the whip,
      And hear the thunder,
        Crack-crack-crack,
          Hear the crack of thunder!

# APPLES

Some people say that Apples are red,
And some people say they're blue.
Here is a blue one for that little boy,
And here is a red one for you.

# THE MIRROR

I look in the Mirror, and what do I see?
A little of you, and a lot of me!

# SPILT MILK: WHODUNIT

Whodunit?
    Who?

"I," said the Crow,
"If you really want to know."

Whodunit?
    Who?

"I," said the Deer,
Grinning ear to ear.

Whodunit?
    Who?

"I," said the Cockatoo,
"Didn't you want me to?"

Whodunit?
    Who?

"I," said the Bear,
"I did it on a dare."

Whodunit?
    Who?

"I," said the Stoat,
Rowing off in a boat.

Whodunit?
Who?

"I," said the Fox,
From under the box.

Whodunit?
Who?

I think it was **YOU**.

# UP THE HILL

Hippety-Hop, goes the Kangaroo,
And the big brown Owl goes, Hoo-Hoo-Hoo!
Hoo-Hoo-Hoo and Hippety-Hop,
Up the Hill, and over the Top!

Baa-Baa-Baa, goes the little white Lamb,
And the Gate that is stuck goes, Jim-Jam-Jam!
Jim-Jam-Jam and Baa-Baa-Baa,
Here we go down again, Tra-La-La!

# THE TOASTER

A silver-scaled Dragon with jaws flaming red
Sits at my elbow and toasts my bread.
I hand him fat slices, and then, one by one,
He hands them back when he sees they are done.

# MOON

I have a white cat whose name is Moon;
He eats catfish from a wooden spoon,
And sleeps till five each afternoon.

Moon goes out when the moon is bright
And sycamore trees are spotted white
To sit and stare in the dead of night.

Beyond still water cries a loon,
Through mulberry leaves peers a wild baboon,
And in Moon's eyes I see the moon.

# MRS. CARIBOU

Old Mrs. Caribou lives by a lake
In the heart of darkest Make-Believe;
She rides through the air on a rickety rake,
And feeds crawfish to a twitchety snake
That sleeps in a basket of African weave.
She sits by the fire when the lights are out
And eats toadstools and sauerkraut,
And bowls of thick white milkweed stew.
If you knock at her door, she will rise and shout,
"Away with you, you roustabout!
My cupboard is bare, my fire is out,
And my door is closed to the likes of you!
Go tie yourself to a hickory stake,
Put a stone on your neck, and jump in the lake.
                    AWAY!"

When the fire burns low and the lights are out
And the moon climbs high above the lake,
And the shutters bang, and the ceilings quake,
Mrs. Caribou comes on her rickety rake
And tries to turn you inside out.
But when she does, what you can do
Is snap your fingers and cry, "Shoo!
Away with YOU, Mrs. Caribou!"
Then she will fly back to Make-Believe
With her snake in a basket of African weave,
And finish her bowl of milkweed stew;

And NEVER come back to bother you.
Shoo, Mrs. Caribou! Shoo, Mrs. Caribou!

Shoo, Mrs. Caribou!

Shoo!

Shoo!

**SHOO!**

# ALICE

There once was a fat little pig named Alice
    Who hated the things that money can buy.
    She wallowed happily in her sty,
While they ate ice cream in the Royal Palace.

# DICTIONARY

A Dictionary's where you can look things up
   To see if they're really there:
        To see if what you breathe is AIR,
        If what you sit on is a CHAIR,
        If what you comb is curly HAIR,
        If what you drink from is a CUP.
A Dictionary's where you can look things up
   To see if they're really there.

# WHEN CANDY WAS CHOCOLATE

When candy was chocolate and bread was white,
When the yellow pencil began to write,
And the hippopotamus said, "Good night!"
My little sister turned out the light.

Then round and round and round in the dark
I dreamt that I sailed on Noah's ark
Past the big blue whale and the hammerhead shark
Round and round and round in the dark.

Round and round until it was light
And beyond the window was land in sight,
Candy was chocolate, bread was white,
And the yellow pencil began to write.

# BIG AND LITTLE

Big boys do,
   Little boys don't.

Big boys will,
   Little boys won't.

Big boys can,
   Little boys can't.

Big boys shall,
   Little boys shan't.

But when little boys
   Are as big as YOU,

Then turn it around
   And it's just as true:

Big boys *don't*,
   Little boys *do*.

# JITTERY JIM

There's room in the bus
For the two of us,
But not for Jittery Jim.

    He has a train
    And a rocket plane,
    He has a seal
    That can bark and swim,
    And a centipede
    With wiggly legs,
    And an ostrich
    Sitting on ostrich eggs,
    And crawfish
    Floating in oily kegs!

There's room in the bus
For the two of us,
But we'll shut the door on *him*!

# MOLLY MOCK-TURTLE

Molly Mock-Turtle of Ocean View
Was stirring a kettle of lobster stew
When she heard in the cupboard a terrible din
As of Kangaroos boxing on roofs of tin,
Or Blue Jays conversing in Mandarin.
She put out her hand for the rolling pin,
Lost her balance, and fell in the stew.
They found her there in Ocean View
Cooked pink as a lobster up to her chin.

# LOVE

I love you, I like you,
I really do like you.
I do *not* want to strike you,
I do *not* want to shove you.
I *do* want to like you,
I *do* want to love you;
And like you and love you
And love you and love you.

# MY BODY

Wherever I go, it also goes,
And when it's dressed, I'm wearing clothes.

# THE PANDA

A lady who lived in Uganda
Was outrageously fond of her Panda:
    With her Chinchilla Cat,
    It ate grasshopper fat
On an air-conditioned veranda.

# GRANDMOTHER
# OSTRICH

Grandmother Ostrich goes to bed
With a towel wrapped around her head;
And even if it's bright as day,
She carries a candle to light her way.

Grandmother Ostrich crosses the sand
To the edge of Never-Never Land;
She looks all about her and sees not a soul,
Then pokes her head in an ostrich hole.

# PICK ME UP

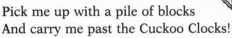

Pick me up with a pile of blocks
And carry me past the Cuckoo Clocks!

Pick me up with a pile of hay
And carry me off to Buzzards Bay!

Pick me up with a pile of snow
And carry me out to Idaho!

Pick me up with a pile of twine
And carry me down to the Argentine!

Pick me up with a pile of lava
And carry me over the hills of Java!

Pick me up with a pile of sand
And put me down in Newfoundland!

# THE QUEEN OF THE NILE

Said the Queen of the Nile
By the green palm tree:
"It is Our desire
That you come to tea
Thursday at twenty-three
Past three
Under the Royal Canopy
In Our Golden Barge
On the River Nile
Beside the Mediterranean
Sea."

I bowed, and said:
"Most certainly!"
To the Queen of the Nile
By the green palm tree.

# FISH

Look at the fish!
Look at the fish!

Look at the fish that is blue and green,
Look at the fish that is tangerine!
Look at the fish that is gold and black
With monocled eye and big humpback!
Look at the fish with the ring in his nose,
And a mouth he cannot open or close!
Look at the fish with lavender stripes
And long front teeth like organ pipes,
And fins that are finer than Irish lace!
Look at that funny grin on his face,
Look at him swimming all over the place!

Look at the fish!
Look at the fish!
*Look* at the fish!
They're so *beautiful*!

# MISTRESS MARY

Mistress Mary, quite contrary,
What can you carry?

Can you carry
A flowerpot?
A platter
Steaming hot?
A blotter
With a blot?
A rope
Tied in a knot?
A lizard
From a grot?
A top-heavy
Whatnot?
A canvas
Army cot?
A leopard cub
Called Spot?
A happy
Hottentot?

Mistress Mary, quite contrary,
*You* can carry
An *awful* lot!

# PEOPLE

Hour after hour,
In many places,
People sit,
Making faces.

# HAVING

A castle has
        a castle moat,
A river has
        a river boat,
An organ has
        an organ note,
A mountain has
        a mountain goat,
But look at my
        new overcoat!

# BETSY ROBIN

Betsy Robin packs her bags,
Picks up all that she can carry,
Then flies away to Kingdom Come
Beyond the tip of Tipperary.

Come back, Betsy, come back home!
We miss you more than anything.
It's always winter when you're gone;
Come back, Betsy, and it's spring!


# THE OWL

The Owl that lives in the old oak tree
Opens his eyes and cannot see
When it's clear as day to you and me;
But not long after the sun goes down
And the Church Clock strikes in Tarrytown
And Nora puts on her green nightgown,
He opens his big bespectacled eyes
And shuffles out of the hollow tree,
And flies and flies
                  and flies and flies,
And flies and flies
                  and flies and flies.

# THINGS

Trains are for going,
Boats are for rowing,
Seeds are for sowing,
Noses for blowing,
    And sleeping's for bed.

Dogs are for pawing,
Logs are for sawing,
Crows are for cawing,
Rivers for thawing,
    And sleeping's for bed.

Flags are for flying,
Stores are for buying,
Glasses for spying,
Babies for crying,
    And sleeping's for bed.

Cows are for mooing,
Chickens for shooing,
Blue is for bluing,
Things are for doing,
    And sleeping's for bed.

Games are for playing,
Hay is for haying,
Horses for neighing,
Saying's for saying,
    And sleeping's for bed.

Money's for spending,
Patients for tending,
Branches for bending,
Poems for ending,
    And sleeping's for bed.

# PUPTENTS AND PEBBLES:

# A Nonsense ABC

"Puptents and Pebbles,"
        Said the King to the Queen;
"The words go together,
        But what do they mean?"

"They make no more sense,"
        Said the Queen with a grin,
"Than a hairbrush of feathers
        Or toothbrush of tin."

The King burst out laughing,
        The Prince came to see;
Then they all read the letters—

**A      B      C      D**

# A is for
# ALPACA

A small woolly llama;
At night to his Mummy
The Alpaca says: "Mama,
Tuck me into my bed
In my woolly pyjama!"

**a** is for **alpaca**

# B is for BATS

At night when the Bats
In their mouse-colored capes
And crumpled-up hats
Fly in through the door,
People scream: "Look out—BATS!"

**b** is for **bats**

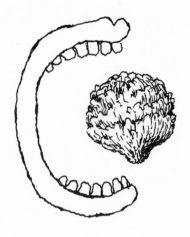

# C is for CABBAGES

Planted in rows,
Each has a green head
But no fingers or toes,
No arms and no legs,
No eyes and no nose.

**c** is for **cabbages**

# D is for DOG

Says the prancing French poodle
As he trots with the band
When it plays "Yankee Doodle":
"Bow-wow! I hate CATS—
The whole kit and caboodle!"

**d** is for **dog**

# E is for EGG

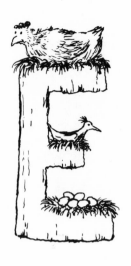

Which the chicken has laid.
From the newly laid Egg
A chicken is made;
By the newly made chicken
A new Egg is laid.

**e** is for **egg**

# F is for
# FROG-BOY

Frog-boy dives in
With mask and frog-flippers
Where parrot fish grin;
And brings up a squid
In an old sardine tin.

**f** is for **frog-boy**

# G is for GOAT

An old Billy Goat
Sang hillbilly songs
As he rowed in a boat;
A fish yanked his beard,
And he hit a high note!

**g** is for **goat**

# H is for HAT

Green, yellow, or red,
Stovepipe or turban,
It sits on your head;
Remove it when bathing
Or when going to bed.

**h** is for **hat**

# I is for
# INKSPOT

A spot of black ink
Looks to you like a yak,
Looks to me like a mink;
An Inkspot can look
Like whatever you think.

**i** is for **inkspot**

# J is for
# JACK-IN-THE-BOX

Flip open the box;
And, a cat from a bag,
Jack *jumps* from the box
With a long paper neck
And no shoes or socks.

**j** is for **jack-in-the-box**

# K is for KING

He says, with a frown,
"My cocoa is cold,
You contemptible clown;
And this upside-down cake
Is NOT upside down!"

**k** is for **king**

# L is for LAUNDRY

The clothes that get clean
In a washtub or basin
Or washing machine;
Then again they get dirty,
And again they get clean.

**l** is for **laundry**

# M is for MASK

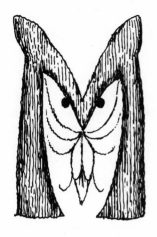

It changes a lot
To add a new face
To the face you have got;
Then the person you are
Is the person you're not.

**m** is for **mask**

# N is for NEEDLE

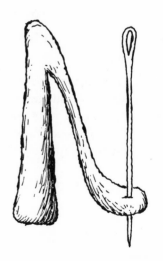

It squinted and said,
"I have only one eye!"
"I have none," said the thread.
"Lend me yours, and we'll sew!"
So they sewed—so they said.

**n** is for **needle**

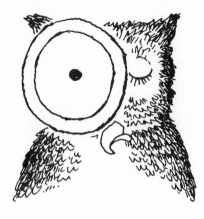

# O is for OWL

The Owl, it is said,
Has eyes he can't move
Without moving his head;
So he lets out a hoot
And stares straight ahead.

**o** is for **owl**

# P is for
# PIRATE

The old buccaneer,
A blade in his teeth,
Remarks, with a sneer,
"Yo—ho—ho! Sailor Boy!
Where's your gold? Hand it here!"

**p** is for **pirate**

# Q is for QUEEN

The Mad Queen in red
Cries, "Button your raincoat!
Off with your head!"
And they say to her, "Ma'am,
Do you *know* what you've said?"

**q** is for **queen**

# R is for REINDEER

In Lapland the Lapps
Drive teams of Reindeer
On the frozen icecaps,
With Reindeer lap rugs
Pulled over their laps.

**r** is for **reindeer**

# S is for SPRINGS

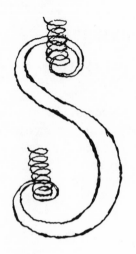

On the Springs in a chair
You wobble, you bounce.
You are here, you are there—
Then, up to no good,
You fly through the air.

**s** is for **springs**

# T is for TUB

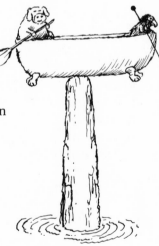

In a Tub one fine day
A pig and a parrot
Went paddling away;
They steered with a clothespin
And sang *Oink! Olé!*

**t** is for **tub**

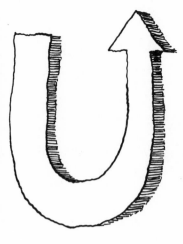

# U is for UP

High Up on the ceiling
I see a house fly.
What can he be feeling
Looking down at his floor
When his floor is the ceiling?

**u** is for **up**

# V is for VOLCANO

A bright mountaintop;
It rumbles and grumbles
Until it can't stop.
With hot rock and ashes
It then blows its top.

**v** is for **volcano**

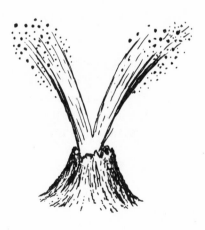

# W is for
# WELL

In the Well is Well water,
And into the Well
Fell the Well-digger's daughter.
Her brother he saved her—
By one foot he caught her!

**w** is for **well**

# X is for X

And X marks the spot
On the rug in the parlor,
The sand in the lot,
Where once you were standing,
And now you are not.

**x** is for **x**

# Y is for YARN

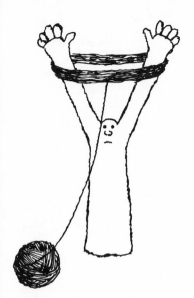

The wool that's unwound
From the ball by the cat
Who bats it around;
And gets it wound up
So it can't be unwound.

**y** is for **yarn**

# Z is for ZEBU

Says the humpbacked Zebu,
"Well, trim my haystack!
Look at me—look at you!
Look again at the letters,
And say them all through!

"Zip-Zip! Zingaroo!
Off your sock!
Off your shoe!
Off to BED now with
YOU!"

**z** is for **zebu**

"Puptents and Pebbles,"
    Said the King to the Queen;
"The words went together,
    But what did they mean?"

"They made no more sense,"
    Said the Queen to the King,
"Than a pet lobster led
    Through the street on a string!

The Prince laughed and laughed
    Till he nodded his head,
And took the book with him
    Upstairs to bed.

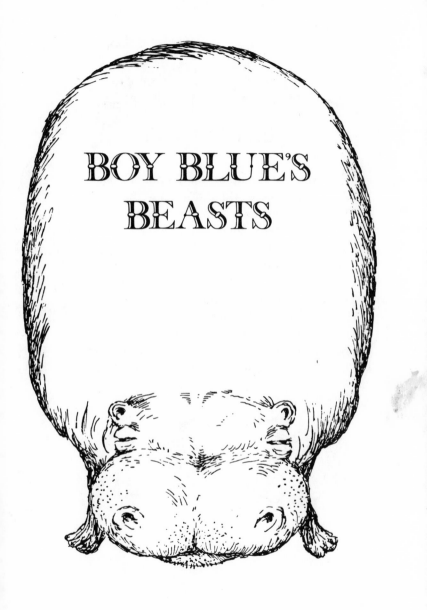

# BOY BLUE'S BEASTS

# ELEPHANT

When you put me up on the Elephant's back,
I'll go round the world and never come back.
I will travel for miles away from home
To London, Paris, Vienna, Rome;
I will journey to India and Siam,
And when people ask me who I am,
I'll say to them all: "My name is Boy Blue.
This is my Elephant; who are you?"
I will ask them all if they'd like to see
The Beasts in my menagerie;
Then if they would, I will show them through
The whole of the world and the whole of the zoo.

# MONKEY

High on a banyan tree in a row
Sat three black Monkeys when it started to snow.
The first Monkey lifted his paw and said:
"I think I must have a cold in the head;
Though snow in a jungle just cannot be,
That certainly looks like snow to me."
The second exclaimed: "I would also
Be inclined to say that it was snow;
But there may be something wrong with me."
Third Monkey—wisest of the three—
Cried: "Look!" and pointed high in the tree.
A fourth Monkey stood there shaking a vine
Heavy with blossoms white and fine
Which fell through the air like flakes of snow
On the upturned faces there below—
And continued to fall till the jungle green
Was changed into a winter scene,
And huge white petals without sound
Had swept in drifts across the ground.

# TIGER

A hunter cried out when he spotted a Tiger,
"What a beautiful rug that creature would make!"
The Tiger growled: he did not agree;
He chased the hunter up a tree.
The hunter's gun went Bang! Bang! Bang!
Zing! Zing! Zing! the bullets sang;
A bunch of bananas plopped to the ground.
The Tiger laughed as he danced around.
He laughed so very hard, poor fellow,
Off flew his stripes of black and yellow.

When lightning flashes through the sky
And the candle glows in my cat's eye;
When thunder rolls from organ pipes,
I think I see those Tiger stripes,
I think I see them whizzing by
In streaks of lightning through the sky.

# YAK

The long-haired Yak has long black hair,
He lets it grow—he doesn't care.
He lets it grow and grow and grow,
He lets it trail along the stair.
Does he ever go to the barbershop? NO!
How wild and woolly and devil-may-care
A long-haired Yak with long black hair
Would look when perched in a barber chair!

# PARROT
## (from Trinidad)

I bought me a Parrot in Trinidad
    And all the Parrot could say
When it got really good and mad,
Was something that sounded terribly bad:

> *Lolloping Lumberjack! Old Baghdad!*
> *Cold Kamchatka! Hot heat pad!*

    But then, when it felt gay,
The Parrot I bought in Trinidad
Would cry with all the voice that it had:

> *Lovely Lollipop! Pink Doodad!*
> *Sweet Elephants!*
> *Hooray!*

# ANTELOPE

When he takes a bath, the Antelope
Uses lots of water and little soap;
Then he shakes himself dry and runs up the slope
As clean as a whistle—or so I hope.

Up the bank quickly the Antelope goes
And on the tall grass he rubs his wet nose.
Down from his ears the cool water flows;
He runs up the bank—and away he goes!

# PIG

Pigs are always awfully dirty;
    I do not think it bothers me.
If I were a Pig, I would say: "My dears,
I do not intend to wash my ears
Once in the next eleven years,
    No matter how dirty they may be!"

Pigs are always awfully muddy;
    I do not think I really care.
If I were a Pig, I would say: "My honeys,
While you stay as clean as the Easter bunnies,
I'll curl in the mud and read the funnies,
    And never, never comb my hair!"

# LION

The Beast that is most fully dressed
Is the Lion in the yellow vest,
The velvet robes of royal red,
A crown of diamonds on his head.
His mane is combed, his paws are clean,
He looks most kingly and serene.
He rises from his royal throne
Beside his golden telephone,
And paces up and down the floor;
He groans, he growls, he starts to roar,
He roars again, he growls some more,
He tears apart his yellow vest,
He takes his robes, his diamond crown,
His telephone, and throws them down,
He kicks them all around the floor.
He gets in such a frightful rage
They have to lock him in a cage
Until he slowly quiets down
And they can give him back his crown,
His velvet robes, his yellow vest,
And he is once more fully dressed.

# CAMEL

The Camel is a long-legged humpbacked beast
With the crumpled-up look of an old worn shoe.
He walks with a creep and a slouch and a slump
As over the desert he carries his hump
Like a top-heavy ship, like a bumper bump-bump.
See him plodding in caravans out of the East,
Bringing silk for a party and dates for a feast.
Is he tired? Is he *thirsty*? No, not in the least.
Good morning, Sir Camel! Good morning to you!

# SEAL

See how he dives
From the rocks with a zoom!
See how he darts
Through his watery room
Past crabs and eels
And green seaweed,
Past fluffs of sandy
Minnow feed!
See how he swims
With a swerve and a twist,
A flip of the flipper,
A flick of the wrist!
Quicksilver-quick,
Softer than spray,
Down he plunges
And sweeps away;
Before you can think,
Before you can utter
Words like "Dill pickle"
Or "Apple butter,"
Back up he swims
Past Sting Ray and Shark,
Out with a zoom,
A whoop, a bark;
Before you can say
Whatever you wish,
He plops at your side
With a mouthful of fish!

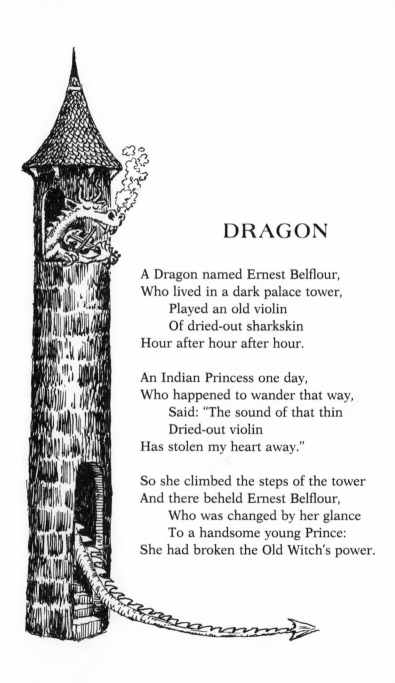

# DRAGON

A Dragon named Ernest Belflour,
Who lived in a dark palace tower,
    Played an old violin
    Of dried-out sharkskin
Hour after hour after hour.

An Indian Princess one day,
Who happened to wander that way,
    Said: "The sound of that thin
    Dried-out violin
Has stolen my heart away."

So she climbed the steps of the tower
And there beheld Ernest Belflour,
    Who was changed by her glance
    To a handsome young Prince:
She had broken the Old Witch's power.

They were married the very next minute
By a neighbor, Sir Larchmont of Linnet,
    And they danced to a thin
    Dried-out violin
Accompanied by a very shrill spinet.

And Ernest said: "Princess, my dear,
I will never blow smoke in your ear,
    No Dragon am I
    But a Prince till I die;
You have nothing whatever to fear.

"Let me buy you some angel food cake
That we'll munch while we walk by the lake,
    Enjoying the smile
    Of the sweet Crocodile,
And the music the Bullfrogs make.

"When a Dragon roars down from the hill,
Having come to do us both ill,
    Belching up flames
    And calling us names,
I will say, 'GO AWAY!' And he will."

# WHALE

When I swam underwater I saw a Blue Whale
Sharing the fish from his dinner pail,
    In an undersea park
    With two Turtles, a Shark,
An Eel, a Squid, and a giant Snail.

When dinner was over, I saw the Blue Whale
Pick up his guests in his dinner pail,
    And swim through the park
    With two Turtles, a Shark,
An Eel, a Squid, and a giant Snail.

# OPOSSUM

Have you ever in your life seen a Possum play
    possum?
Have you ever in your life seen a Possum play
    dead?
When a Possum is trapped and can't get away
He turns up his toes and lays down his head,
Bats both his eyes and rolls over dead.
But then when you leave him and run off to play,
The Possum that really was just playing possum
Gets up in a flash and scurries away.

# UNICORN

The Unicorn with the long white horn
    Is beautiful and wild.
He gallops across the forest green
So quickly that he's seldom seen
Where Peacocks their blue feathers preen
    And strawberries grow wild.
He flees the hunter and the hounds,
Upon black earth his white hoof pounds,
Over cold mountain streams he bounds
    And comes to a meadow mild;
There, when he kneels to take his nap,
He lays his head in a lady's lap
    As gently as a child.

# KANGAROO

A tough Kangaroo named Hopalong Brown
Boxed all the badmen out of town.
When he came hopping back home one day,
They presented him with a big bouquet
And named him the Champion of Animal Town.
Hip, Hip, Hooray for Hopalong Brown!

Three cheers for the Champion, Hopalong Brown!
(All of you badmen, get out of town!)
Three cheers for his wife, Mrs. Hopalong Crockett,
And the Hopalong kiddies tucked in her pocket!
Long may he wear his Tumbleweed Crown,
Three cheers for the Champion, Hopalong Brown!

*Hip*
　　*Hip*
　　　　*Hooray!*
*Hip*　*Hip*
　　　*Hooray!*
*Hip*
　　*Hip*
　　HOORAY!

# HEN

The little red Hen does not write with a pen,
She uses her feet to scratch in the clay.
To me the hen-scratching looks like Greek
Or Turkish, which I cannot speak.
What on earth is she trying to say?

Is she trying to say that the leaves are turning,
The sky is falling, the toast is burning,
That worms have got into her chicken feed?
Around her, yellow fluffs of sun,
The little chickens chirp and run,
And whatever she writes, they rush to read.

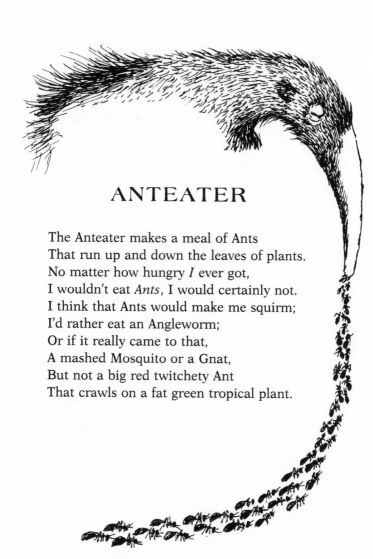

# ANTEATER

The Anteater makes a meal of Ants
That run up and down the leaves of plants.
No matter how hungry *I* ever got,
I wouldn't eat *Ants*, I would certainly not.
I think that Ants would make me squirm;
I'd rather eat an Angleworm;
Or if it really came to that,
A mashed Mosquito or a Gnat,
But not a big red twitchety Ant
That crawls on a fat green tropical plant.

# MOLE

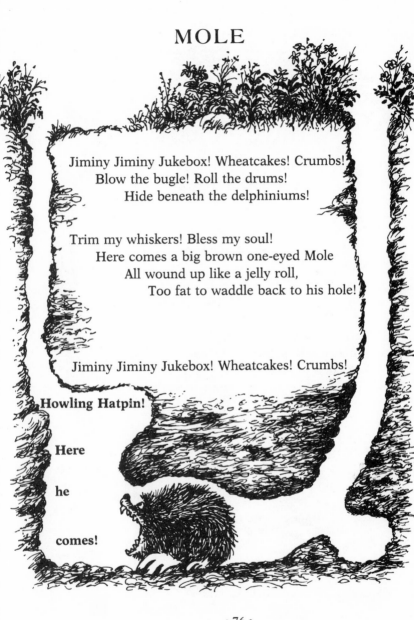

Jiminy Jiminy Jukebox! Wheatcakes! Crumbs!
Blow the bugle! Roll the drums!
Hide beneath the delphiniums!

Trim my whiskers! Bless my soul!
Here comes a big brown one-eyed Mole
All wound up like a jelly roll,
Too fat to waddle back to his hole!

Jiminy Jiminy Jukebox! Wheatcakes! Crumbs!

**Howling Hatpin!**

**Here**

**he**

**comes!**

# RHINOCEROS

You may hang your hat on the nose of the Rhino—
    There's really no better place for your hat—
But leave your overcoat in the closet,
    And wipe your feet on the front-door mat.

You may hang your hat on the nose of the Rhino,
    That's what the Rhino's nose is for;
But do not whoop when you cross the hallway
    And troop like wild men through the door.

Don't dance along the warpath, grunting, swaying,
    In the jungle you have found beneath those chairs,
Or the Rhino may forget you're only playing,
    And *charge*—and chase you all downstairs.

# COATI-MUNDI

As I went walking one fine Sunday,
I happened to meet a Coati-Mundi.
    "Coati-Mundi," I said,
    "It's a lovely Sunday
As sure as you're a Coati-Mundi,
A handsome long-tailed Coati-Mundi
    With eyes peering out,
    A flexible snout,
And a raccoon coat all furry and bundly!"

"I quite agree," said the Coati-Mundi,
"It is indeed a most beautiful Sunday.
    What joy for the eye!
    What clouds! What sky!
    What fields of rye!
    Oh, never have I
In all my life seen such a Sunday!"

So he took my hand, and we walked together,
I and my friend, the Coati-Mundi,
Enjoying that most unusual weather,
Enjoying that most delightful Sunday.

# ZEBRA

Are Zebras black with broad white stripes,
Or are they really white with black?
Answer me that and I'll give you some candy
And a green-and-yellow jumping jack.

The finest animal I know
Is the good black Water Buffalo.
When the sun of the East beats down on the clay
And coconuts fall and palm trees sway,
He plods through the rice field day after day.
With graceful long horns, he is gentle and slow:
I love the Water Buffalo!

# GOONEY BIRD

The silliest fowl, the most absurd,
Is certainly the Gooney Bird.
When a Gooney tumbles to the ground
All he will do is flop around,
Roll his dumbbell eyes and stare
Off into the empty air.
Of silly fowl I know another—
The Booby Bird, the Gooney's brother.
The Dodo, too, that's found no more
In Mozambique or Singapore.
Dead is the Dodo, gone is the Auk
That couldn't fly but only walk.
Gooney Bird, Booby Bird, Dodo, Auk,
Don't let me hear that silly talk—
Come on, Gooney, get up and try
To flap your clumsy wings and fly!

# BUTTERFLY

Of living creatures most I prize
Black-spotted yellow Butterflies
Sailing softly through the skies,

Whisking light from each sunbeam,
Gliding over field and stream—
Like fans unfolding in a dream,

Like fans of gold lace flickering
Before a drowsy elfin king
For whom the thrush and linnet sing—

Soft and beautiful and bright
As hands that move to touch the light
When Mother leans to say good night.

# CROCODILE

The Crocodile wept bitter tears,
  And when I asked him why,
He said: "I weep because the years
  Go far too quickly by!

"I weep because of oranges,
  I weep because of pears,
Because of broken door hinges,
  And dark and crooked stairs.

"I weep because of black shoestrings,
  I weep because of socks,
I weep because I can't do things
  Like dance and shadowbox.

"I weep because the deep blue sea
  Washes the sand in a pile;
I weep because, as you can see,
  I've never learned to smile!"

"To weep like that cannot be fun,
  My reptile friend," I said;
"Your nose, though long, will run and run,
  Your eyes, though wide, be red.

"Why must you so give way to grief?
  You *could* smile if you chose;
Here, take this pocket handkerchief
  And wipe your eyes and nose.

"Come, laugh because of oranges,
     And laugh because of pears,
Because of broken door hinges,
     And dark and crooked stairs.

"Come, laugh because of black shoestrings,
     And laugh because of socks,
And laugh because you *can* do things
     Like dance and shadowbox.

"Come, laugh because it feels so good—
     It's not against the law.
Throw open, as a reptile should,
     Your green and shining jaw!"

The Crocodile he thought awhile
     Till things seemed not so black;
He smiled, and I returned his smile,
     He smiled, and I smiled back.

He took an orange and a pear;
     He took shoestrings and socks,
And, tossing them into the air,
     Began to waltz and box.

The animals came, and they were gay:
     The Bobcat danced with the Owl;
The Bat brought tea on a bamboo tray
     To the Yak and Guinea Fowl.

The Monkeys frolicked in the street;
     The Lion, with a smile,
Came proudly down the steps to greet
     The happy Crocodile!

# TAPIR

How odd it would be if ever a Tapir,
Wrapped in gold and silver paper
And tied with a bow in the shape of a T,
Sat there in the corner beside the tree
When I tiptoed down at six in the morning—
A Christmas present from you to me!

Into the town then we would caper,
I and the ugly, pink-nosed Tapir,
And people would gather round to see.
They would publish our picture in the paper,
And, with it, the words:

## BOY BLUE AND THE TAPIR
## THAT HE FOUND BENEATH
## HIS CHRISTMAS TREE

# HIPPOPOTAMUS

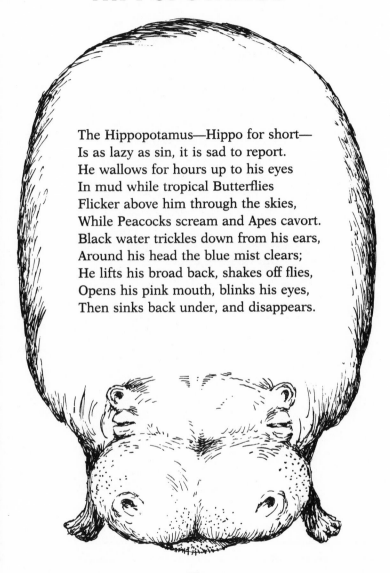

The Hippopotamus—Hippo for short—
Is as lazy as sin, it is sad to report.
He wallows for hours up to his eyes
In mud while tropical Butterflies
Flicker above him through the skies,
While Peacocks scream and Apes cavort.
Black water trickles down from his ears,
Around his head the blue mist clears;
He lifts his broad back, shakes off flies,
Opens his pink mouth, blinks his eyes,
Then sinks back under, and disappears.

# CAT

Cats are not at all like people,
  Cats are Cats.

People wear stockings and sweaters,
Overcoats, mufflers, and hats.
Cats wear nothing: they lie by the fire
For twenty-four hours if they desire.
They do NOT rush out to the office,
They do NOT have interminable chats,
They do NOT play Old Maid and Checkers,
They do NOT wear bright yellow spats.

People, of course, will always be people,
  But Cats are Cats.

# DOG

Dogs are quite a bit like people,
    Or so it seems to me somehow.
Like people, Dogs go anywhere,
They swim in the sea, they leap through the air,
They bark and growl, they sit and stare,
They even wear what people wear.
Look at that Poodle with a hat on its noodle,
Look at that Boxer in a long silver-fox fur,
Look at that Whippet in its calico tippet,
Look at that Sealyham in diamonds from Rotterdam,
Look at that Afghan wrapped in an afghan,
Look at that Chow down there on a dhow
All decked out for some big powwow
With Pekinese waiting to come kowtow.
    Don't they all look just like people?
    People you've *seen* somewhere? Bowwow!

# FOX AND CROW

High in the flowering catalpa trees,
Sir Crow in his beak held a large hunk of cheese.
Sir Fox, by its fragrance drawn that way,
Felt himself called upon to say:
"Allow me, Black Majesty, to suggest
That if the wealth of your dark vest
Is matched in fullness by your song,
I cannot think that I am wrong—
You must be a singer beyond compare!"
These words to the Crow were sweet to hear,
And, swelling with pride, he flung open his craw,
Emitting a most lugubrious *Caw!*
Down through the branches tumbled the cheese,
Which the Fox gobbled up with the greatest of ease
As he trotted beneath the catalpa trees.

You can swim with a pocket stuffed with rocks
Sooner than you can believe a Fox;
And do *not* try to do what you cannot do
No matter who may want you to!

# COW

Cows are not supposed to fly,
  And so, if you should see
    A spotted Cow go flying by
    Above a pawpaw tree
In a porkpie hat with a green umbrella,
  Then run right down the road and tell a
    Lady selling sarsaparilla,
    Lemon soda and vanilla,
So she can come here and tell me!

# PARROT
## (from Zambezi)

A Parrot I bought in Zambezi
Would perch, while I played Parcheesi,
With feathers all ruffled and breezy,
And ask in a voice that was wheezy:

*Boy Blue, is it hot?*

*Boy Blue, is it hot?*

To that Parrot I bought in Zambezi
That perched, while I played Parcheesi,
With feathers all ruffled and breezy,
I replied—and it was quite easy—

*Certainly not!*

*Certainly not!*

*Certainly not even half as hot*

*As it is*

*On the streets of Zambezi!*

# GULL

Life is seldom if ever dull
For the lazy long-winged white Sea Gull.
　　It is as interesting as can be;
He lies on the wind, a slender reed,
And wheels and dips for hours to feed
On scruffy fish and pickleweed
　　And to smell the smell of the sea.

He wheels and dips: beneath his wings
The pirate grins, the sailor sings,
　　As they ply the China Sea.
While cold winds grip a schooner's sail
And water spouts from a great White Whale,
Perched on a mast, he rides the gale—
　　What a wonderful life has he!

# RACCOON

One summer night a little Raccoon,
Above his left shoulder, looked at the new moon.
    He made a wish;
    He said: "I wish
    I were a Catfish,
    A Blowfish, a Squid,
    A Katydid,
    A Beetle, a Skink,
    An Ostrich, a pink
    Flamingo, a Gander,
    A Salamander,
    A Hippopotamus,
    A Duck-billed Platypus,
    A Gecko, a Slug,
    A Water Bug,
    A pug-nosed Beaver,
    Anything whatever
Except what I am, a little Raccoon!"

Above his left shoulder, the Evening Star
Listened and heard the little Raccoon
    Who wished on the moon;
    And she said: "Why wish
    You were a Catfish,
    A Blowfish, a Squid,
    A Katydid,
    A Beetle, a Skink,
    An Ostrich, a pink
    Flamingo, a Gander,
    A Salamander,
    A Hippopotamus,

A Duck-billed Platypus,
A Gecko, a Slug,
A Water Bug,
A pug-nosed Beaver,
Anything whatever?
Why must you change?" said the Evening Star,
"When you are perfect as you are?
I know a boy who wished on the moon
That *he* might be a little Raccoon!"

# PENGUIN

I think it must be very nice
To stroll about upon the ice,
Night and day, day and night,
Wearing only black and white,
Always in your Sunday best—
Black tailcoat and pearl-white vest.
To stroll about so pleasantly
Beside the cold and silent sea
Would really suit me to a T!
I think it must be very nice
To stroll with Penguins on the ice.

*For those who like the Arctic air,*
*There also is the Polar Bear.*

# POLAR BEAR

The Polar Bear never makes his bed;
He sleeps on a cake of ice instead.
He has no blanket, no quilt, no sheet
Except the rain and snow and sleet.
He drifts about on a white ice floe
While cold winds howl and blizzards blow
And the temperature drops to forty below.
The Polar Bear never makes his bed;
The blanket he pulls up over his head
Is lined with soft and feathery snow.
If ever he rose and turned on the light,
He would find a world of bathtub white,
And icebergs floating through the night.

# GIRAFFE

When I invite the Giraffe to dine,
I ask a carpenter friend of mine
To build a table so very tall
It takes up nearly the whole front hall.
The Giraffe and I do not need chairs:
He stands—I sit on the top of the stairs;
And we eat from crisp white paper plates
A meal of bananas, figs, and dates.

He whispers, when the table's clear,
Just loud enough for me to hear:
"Come one day soon to dine with me
And sit high up in a banyan tree
While Beasts of earth and sea and air
Gather all around us there,
All around the Unicorn
Who leads them with his lowered horn—

"And we'll eat *without* white paper plates
A meal of bananas, figs, and dates."

# SWAN

"You have seen the world, you have seen the zoo,
And the lovely animals," said Boy Blue.
"I am weary now and I long to fly
Round and round in the big blue sky;
And wouldn't you, too, if you were I?"
So he called to the Swan on the edge of the stream,
And the Swan floated up like a ship in a dream,
A ship with billowing sails of white
To take him far into the night.
He climbed on its back, and away they flew.
The children said, "Good-bye! Good-bye!"
"Good-bye to you all!" replied Boy Blue.

# THE
# OLD MAN
# FROM
# OKEFENOKEE:
## Loony and
## Lopsided Limericks

There was an Old Man from Luray
Who always had something to say;
  But each time he tried
  With his mouth opened wide
His big tongue would get in the way.

There was a Young Person named Crockett
Who attached himself to a rocket;
  He flew out through space
  At such a great pace
That his pants flew out of his pocket.

There was an Old Lady named Brown
Who whisked a large fan around town;
  Which might have been good
  Had it not been of wood
And used freely to knock people down.

An Old Man from Okefenokee
Liked to sing in a most dismal low key;
  He would perch on a log
  And boom like a frog
Through the dark swamp of Okefenokee.

There was an Old Lady named Hart,
Whose appearance gave people a start:
    Her shape was a candle's,
    Her ears like door handles,
And her front teeth three inches apart.

There was an Old Lady named Crockett
Who went to put a plug in a socket;
    But her hands were so wet
    She flew up like a jet
And came roaring back down like a rocket!


There was an Old Woman named Piper
Who spoke like a windshield wiper.
    She would say: "Dumb Gump!
    Wet Stump! Wet Stump!"
And then like the voice of disaster
Her words would come faster and faster:
    "Dumb Gump! Dumb Gump!
    Wet Stump! Wet Stump!
    Wet Stump! Wet Stump!
Tiddledy-diddledy-diddledy-bump . . .
        Bump . . .
            Bump . . .
                Bump . . .
                    BUMP!"
—Which greatly annoyed *Mr.* Piper!

There was a Young Lady named Rose
Who was constantly blowing her nose;
    Because of this failing
    They sent her off whaling
So the whalers could say: "Thar she blows!"


A Young Man from Old Terre Haute
Had a string of six catfish he'd caught.
    While he lingered to chat,
    They attracted a cat,
Which reduced the six catfish to naught.


A contentious Old Person named Reagan,
Who lived in the heart of Skowhegan,
    Would get in a dither,
    And then on a zither
Play tunes that were dull and fatiguin'.


An obnoxious Old Person named Hackett
Bought a huge trunk and started to pack it.
    When he tripped and fell in it
    And it shut the next minute,
He proceeded to make quite a racket.

A Matron well known in Montclair
Was never quite sure what to wear.
    Once when very uncertain
    She put on a lace curtain
And ran a bell cord through her hair.


There was a Young Man on a plain
Who wandered about in the rain.
    He said: "Well, what OF it?
    I LOVE it! I LOVE it!"
And he said so again and again.


There was an Old Woman named Ware
Whose pearls got caught in her hair.
    While setting them free,
    She was chased up a tree
By a dachshund that growled like a bear.


There was a Young Lady named Groat
Whose pleasure it was to emote.
    She would say with a tear,
    "I am not wanted here!"
Then get up and take off her coat.

There was an Old Woman named Porter
Who swam with her head under water.
    One could see from the shore
    Her two feet, nothing more—
Which was almost too much for her daughter.

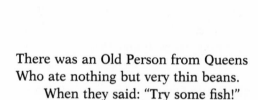

There was an Old Person from Queens
Who ate nothing but very thin beans.
    When they said: "Try some fish!"
    He pooh-poohed them: "Tish!"
So they smashed him to smithereens.

There was a Young Man from Alassio
Who put his foot down on the gas-i-o—
    Smashed into a tree,
    Ended up in the sea—
And was never seen more in Alassio!

A Lady whose name was Miss Hartley
Understood most things only partly.
    When they said: "Get this straight,"
    She said: "What?—What?—What?—WAIT!"
So they had to give up with Miss Hartley.

There was an Old Man from the Coast
Who once, while acting as host,
    Said: "Will you have peas
    With buttered car keys?
. . . Or sawdust with cinnamon toast?"


A Mother in Old Alabama
Said: "I declare, what a clamor!
    Little Beulah Louise
    Cut down those pine trees
With Big Brother's chisel and hammer!"


An eccentric explorer named Hayter
Sat down on an alligator;
    In the swamp in the fog
    It resembled a log.
Exploration thus ended for Hayter.

A querulous Cook from Pomona,
One day while attempting to bone a
    Tough chicken, went wild
    And chased his grandchild
Up a tree in a park in Pomona.


There was an Old Man from Japan
Who rolled down the hill in a can;
    He was carted away
    The very next day
By some men in a moving van.


Young radical Byron McNally
Marched off in a mob to a rally,
    And with red flag held high,
    Eyes fixed on the sky,
Headed straight for an awful blind alley.

A Captain, retired from the Navy,
Lived on mashed potatoes and gravy.
   He stood with an oar
   And stared at the floor,
Reflecting at length on the Navy.


There was an Old Man of Toulon
Who never had anything on.
   When they said: "Wear some clothes!"
   He inquired: "What are those?"
So they chased that man out of Toulon.


A bicycle rider named Crockett
With a homemade gas bomb in his pocket
   Just happened to scratch
   The bomb with a match;
All that's left of his bike is one sprocket.


There was an Old Lady from Java
Who said, as she chewed on a guava,
   "Broken bucket, green bean it,
   Donkey doodle—I mean it!"
So they shipped her by jet back to Java.

There was an Old Man by Salt Lake
Who exclaimed when but partly awake:
    "Hi-di-diddle bum nickel
    Gum bubble tricycle!"
And they said: "Aw, go jump in the lake!"

There was an Old Person who said,
Pointing out the oil lamp on his head:
    "It perhaps does not pay
    During most of the day,
But it's helpful when reading in bed!"

There was an Old Woman from Winnipeg
Who had a big foot but so thin a leg
    That all she could do
    When she put on a shoe
Was to weave like a willow in Winnipeg.

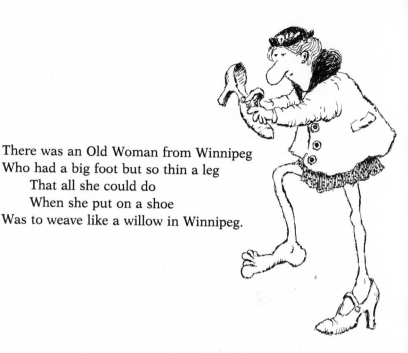

Two revolting Young Persons named Gruen
Always did what they shouldn't be doin'.
    When their Ma cried, "Don't do it!"
    Got a whistle and blew it,
They just did what they shouldn't be doin'.


An abhorrent Young Person named Plunkett
Had an old car and went off to junk it;
    On the edge of the dump
    The car hit a bump
And into the dump it hurled Plunkett.

# BROOKLYN BRIDGE

# A VISIT TO THE MAYOR

I went to see the Mayor at City Hall,
And he said, "Hello," but that wasn't all.

He said, "Good morning!" and "How do you do?
Did you ride on the ferry? Have you been to the zoo?

"Do you have a pet dog? Or a bird? Or a cat?
And what will you be—have you thought about that?

"Have you thought when you grow up one day what you
Will want to be then? What you'll want to do?

"Will you fly an airplane, sail an ocean liner,
Be a taxi driver, a dress designer?

"Will you dress up in white and look after the sick,
Or work at a switchboard: 'Number, please—click!'

"Be a butcher, a baker, dog trainer, or farmer,
A tightrope walker or a snake charmer?

"An architect, a builder of bridges,
A gardener's assistant, a trimmer of hedges?

"A detective who solves a terrible crime
In the Case of the Lazy Man Who Killed Time?

"There are so many things in the world to do:
Which of them all will appeal to you?"

Then I said, "When I'm twenty or twenty-nine,
I will come back and tell you." And he said, "That's fine."

He picked up his gloves and put on his hat
And he said, "Good-bye, I've enjoyed our chat."

I went to see the Mayor at City Hall,
And he said, "Hello," but that wasn't all.

# BROOKLYN BRIDGE
## *A Jump-rope Rhyme*

Brooklyn Bridge, Brooklyn Bridge,
I walked to the middle, jumped over the edge.
The water was greasy, the water was brown
Like cold chop suey in Chinatown.
And I gobbled it up as I sank down—
       Down—
          Down—
             Down—
                Down—

Brooklyn Bridge, Brooklyn Bridge,
I walked to the middle, looked over the edge.
But I didn't jump off, what I said's not true—
I just made it up so I could scare you:
       Watch me jump!—
          Watch me jump!—
             Watch me jump!—
             BOO!

# SUBWAY CENTIPEDE

The Subway Centipede, slots in its side,
Flings open the slots so people may ride,
And roars for miles through an Elephant's hide
And tunnels down through his Ivory Tusks,
And feeds on swill and peanut husks.

Here comes the nearsighted thousand-legger,
Reeling like a carpetbagger,
Roaring so fast it makes you stagger!

See!

S-E-E-E-E-E-E-E-E-E-E-E-E-E-E!

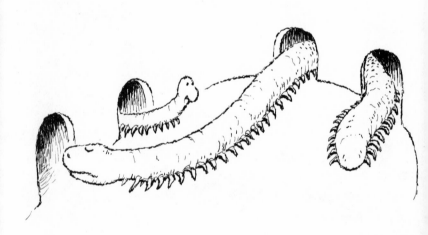

# KING KONG BAT

"Anything wrong?"
Cries the hairy King Kong
As it flies along.

"I'll fetch you, mate,
And carry you straight
To the very top
Of the Empire State
And sing you a song
(You can sing along):

" 'Anything wrong?
Forget your worries;
For Life is a bowl
Of plastic cherries,
A sumptuous treat
On a one-way street;
It begins with a Howl
And ends with a Bong . . .
                    Bong . . .
                            Bong . . .

Anything wrong?' "

# THE EASTER PARADE

What shall I wear for the Easter Parade?
A dress that's the color of marmalade
With a border embroidered in light blue cornflowers
Like the edge of a meadow after spring showers
And a matching hat round as a top you can spin
And elastic to hold it on under my chin
And brand-new shoes whiter than newly poured cream
With heart-shaped, golden buckles that gleam;
And I'll carry a small purse of butterfly blue
With a penny for me and a penny for you
To buy us both glasses of cold lemonade
When we walk, hand in hand, in the Easter Parade.

# BAY-BREASTED
# BARGE BIRD

The Bay-Breasted Barge Bird delights in depressions
And simply flourishes during slumps;
It winters on hummocks near used-car lots
    And summers near municipal dumps.

It nests on the coils of old bedsprings,
And lines its nest with the labels from cans;
It feeds its young on rusty red things;
    And bits of pots and pans.

The Bay-Breasted Barge Bird joyfully passes
Where bulldozers doze and wreckers rumble,
Gazing bug-eyed, when traffic masses,
    At buildings that feather and crumble.

It flaps long wings the color of soot,
It cranes a neck dotted with purple bumps;
And lets out a screech like a car in a crack-up
    As it slowly circles the dumps.

# THE GREASE MONKEY
# AND THE POWDER PUFF

**Grease Monkey:** *slang expression for* **Garage Mechanic**.
**Powder Puff:** *slang expression for* **Prize Fighter**.

The Grease Monkey said to the Powder Puff,
"I'm sick of your grousin', fed up with your guff.
You think you can fight—well, I'm callin' your bluff.
Wipe that smile off your face like a streak of goose fat;
I may grease your car but I'm not takin' that."
Then the Grease Monkey knocked the Powder Puff flat.

# IMAGINARY
# DIALOGUES

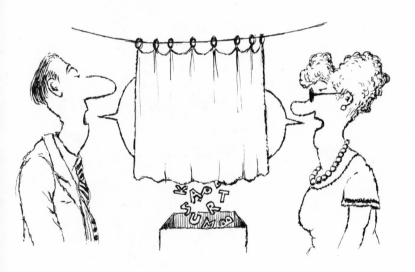

Said Ogden Nash to Phyllis McGinley,
"I like my ham sliced rather thinly."
"I'd slice it for you, but I must dash!"
Said Phyllis McGinley to Ogden Nash.


Said Dorothy Hughes to Helen Hocking,
"I can't for the life of me get on this stocking!"
"Would it help if you first removed your shoes?"
Said Helen Hocking to Dorothy Hughes.

Said Marcia Brown to Carlos Baker,
"I can't get salt from this saltshaker!"
"Just try turning it upside down!"
Said Carlos Baker to Marcia Brown.


Said General Shoup to Adja Yunkers,
"I hate the sight of doughnut dunkers!"
"They're better than people who blow in their soup!"
Said Adja Yunkers to General Shoup.


Said Arlene Francis to Granville Hicks,
"Shall we bake a cake with this cake mix?"
"I shouldn't care to take such chances,"
Said Granville Hicks to Arlene Francis.


Said Justice Douglas to Douglass Cater,
"Look at that butter-fingered waiter!"
"This place will soon be a glass or mug less!"
Said Douglass Cater to Justice Douglas.

# A
# CLUTCH
# OF
# CLERIHEWS

Edmund Clerihew Bentley,
Looking at his name one day intently,
Found it contained that very new
Verse form, the clerihew.


William Penn
Was the most levelheaded of men;
He had only one mania—
Pennsylvania.


Beatrix Potter,
While doodling with her pen on a fuzzy blotter,
May well have developed the habit
Of drawing Peter Rabbit.


Sir Walter Raleigh
Never rode on a trolley;
But he took many a long trip
By ship.

What difference did it make to Longfellow
Whether his necktie was the right or the wrong yellow
Since when he appeared
It was hidden by his beard?

Lady Hester Stanhope
Said, "With Arabs I think I can cope."
Then, feeling rather grand,
She galloped off in a cloud of sand.

# A
# NUTHATCH
# OF
# NONSENSE BIRDS

# CHIT-CHAT

On a broad-brimmed hat
Sits the tiny Chit-Chat;
And it sings: Chit-Chat!
What of that? What of that?
And it sings: Chit-Chat!
    What of that?

# FAUCET

By the shape of the beak, if not the size,
The Faucet is simple to recognize.

# COLLECTOR BIRD

The Collector, I am told, exists
On old waste paper and laundry lists
And a few dried prunes it salts away
In a bottom drawer for a rainy day.

# CAT-WHISKERED CATBIRD

When it spreads its wings and doffs its hat
You would swear the Canary had swallowed the Cat!

# HACKLE BIRD

When the Hackle Bird
Gets up its hackles,
It clucks and clucks,
It cackles and cackles;
It beats the air,
It hollers and hoots,
Stomps on young trees,
Tears them up by the roots;
Runs down the mountain,
Dives through the brake,
Holds its breath—
And jumps in the lake.

# PIGEON-TOED PIGEONS

Pigeon-toed Pigeons on the grass, alas!


# HOOLIE BIRD

The Hoolie Bird now is almost extinct;
When last reported there were three.
If in some dark corner of your precinct,
You come on a Hoolie, let him be!


# SLANT-EYED PEEKER

The Slant-eyed Peeker sits on a low bough,
And peeks through a keyhole—*there* he is now!

# DOLLAR BIRD

The Dollar Bird lives
Between two boards;
And feathers its nest
With the money it hoards.

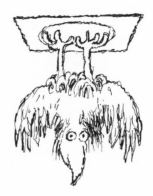

# UPSIDE-DOWN BIRD

The Upside-Down Bird hangs from the ceiling,
Its eyes shut tight and its beak dangling down—
A feat which, although not really appealing,
Has earned for the bird a certain renown.

# COMMON
# MUDLATCH

The Common Mudlatch,
Found in any weed patch,
Latches on to the mud
Until its eggs hatch.
Then, turning handsprings,
Distracted it flings
Both mud-laden wings
And plasters with mud
Every inch of its patch.

# POSTMAN PELICAN

In the pouch of the ambling Postman Pelican
Are hundreds of letters which he delivers,
Or takes out somewhere and quietly buries,
Or chews and swallows or throws into rivers;
Or takes home and keeps for months and months—
And *then* delivers.

# GONDOLA SWAN

A most graceful bird is the Gondola Swan,
It feeds on love letters and old lemon rinds;
And lowers its neck like a long melting candle,
And raises its wings like Venetian blinds.

# EXECUTIVE EAGLE

From dawn until dusk
When the dogwood's in flower,
It sits by the highway
And screams: "Eisenhower!"

It screams with delight
And with rare vocal power:
"Coolidge! Taft! Truman!
Roosevelt! Eisenhower!"

# TELEVISION TOUCAN

The Television Toucan,
When given a pecan,
Will jiggle and belch,
Sing in Urdu and Welsh,
Jump, jitter, and jimmy,
Squirm, skitter, and shimmy,
Croak, quiver, and quake,
Till your eyes have popped out
And all your bones ache.

# HORN-RIMMED HEN

The Horn-rimmed Hen
Remains on the stoop
When the lights go out
In the chicken coop;
When the Milky Way
Climbs above the milkweed,
And the planets gather
Like chicken feed.

# RAGE

With cauliflower ear
And shiny black eye,
The Rage is flown into;
It cannot fly.

# DRESSMAKING SCREAMER

The Dressmaking Screamer,
As it rips out the seams,
Spits pins and needles,
And screams!—screams!

# ZIPPER BIRD

The Zipper Bird goes Zip-Zip! Zip-Zip!
And zooms across the lawn.
Zip! goes the Zipper up through the trees,
And Zip! the Zipper is gone!

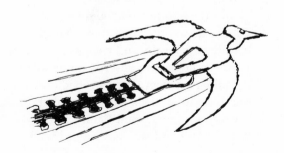

# WALKING-STICK BIRD

The Walking-Stick Bird, of which few have heard,
Does nothing under the sun but walk.
It cannot sing, it cannot talk,
It seldom eats, it never flies.
It walks and walks and walks and walks;
It walks on roads and on sidewalks,
It walks past bushes, stems, and stalks,
It walks down railroads, past road signs,
Past blinking lights and yellow lines,
Past supermarkets, skating rinks,
Bowling alleys and golf links,
It walks past ladies with mink stoles,
Past barbershops with bright pink poles,
And miners working in sinkholes;
It walks down lanes, through fields of clover,
Under underpasses, over
Bridges, in and out of doors,
Round and round and round dance floors;
It walks through woods, it walks by streams,
And never stops and never dreams
Of sitting down to take the air;
It walks along a thoroughfare
That joins another thoroughfare
That joins another one somewhere;
It walks for weeks and weeks and weeks
Through hot white deserts, up white peaks,
It walks past men with tattooed cheeks
And blood-red birds with soup-plate beaks;
It walks on far beyond Land's End,
Where sand and sky and water blend;

It walks past oceans yet uncharted,
And when it gets back where it started,
It looks around it, blinks its eyes,
Then, as if taken by surprise,
Screams Bloody Murder, crumples up, and dies.

# NONSENSE
# COOKERY

# CANAPÉS À LA POSTE

Pit two dozen black olives and stuff with canceled and shredded postage stamps.

Drop the stuffed olives in the nearest mailbox. Then decide on your next course.

# HOT AND COLD TIN-CAN SURPRISE

You will need a dozen assorted unlabeled cans of varied shapes and sizes from your local supermarket.

Place a half dozen of the cans in your deep-freeze; drop the other half dozen in kettles of boiling water.

Forget; and allow to boil and freeze for an indefinite period.

Serve one hot and one cold can to each of your guests with individual can openers.

If they aren't surprised, you will know what to label them.

*You may wish to follow*
*Hot and Cold Tin-Can Surprise with:*

# CHOCOLATE
# MOOSE

Take, if you can, a Moose.
Brush with chocolate.
Move your Moose into the dining room.
Then watch your party break up.

# THE FLOOR
# AND
# THE CEILING

# THE FLOOR
# AND THE CEILING

Winter and summer, whatever the weather,
The Floor and the Ceiling were happy together
In a quaint little house on the outskirts of town
With the Floor looking up and the Ceiling looking down.

The Floor bought the Ceiling an ostrich-plumed hat,
And they dined upon drippings of bacon fat,
Diced artichoke hearts and cottage cheese
And hundreds of other such delicacies.

On a screened-in porch in early spring
They would sit at the player piano and sing.
When the Floor cried in French, *"Ah, je vous adore!"*
The Ceiling replied, "You adorable Floor!"

The years went by as the years they will,
And each little thing was fine until
One evening, enjoying their bacon fat,
The Floor and the Ceiling had a terrible spat.

The Ceiling, loftily looking down,
Said, "You are the *lowest* Floor in this town!"
The Floor, looking up with a frightening grin,
Said, "Keep up your chatter, and *you* will cave in!"

So they went off to bed: while the Floor settled down,
The Ceiling packed up her gay wallflower gown;
And tiptoeing out past the Chippendale chair
And the gateleg table, down the stair,

Took a coat from the hook and a hat from the rack,
And flew out the door—farewell to the Floor!—
And flew out the door, and was seen no more,
And flew out the door, and *never* came back!

In a quaint little house on the outskirts of town,
Now the shutters go bang, and the walls tumble down;
And the roses in summer run wild through the room,
But blooming for no one—then why should they bloom?

For what is a Floor now that brambles have grown
Over window and woodwork and chimney of stone?
For what is a Floor when the Floor stands alone?
And what is a Ceiling when the Ceiling has flown?

# LITTLE DIMITY

Poor little pigeon-toed Dimity Drew,
The more she ate, the smaller she grew.
When some people eat, they get taller and taller;
When Dimity ate, she got smaller and smaller.
She went for a walk, and all you could see
Was a tam-o'-shanter the size of a pea,
An umbrella as big as the cross on a *t*,
And a wee pocketbook of butterfly blue.
She came to a crack one half an inch wide,
Tripped on a bread crumb, fell inside,
And slowly disappeared from view.

# BIG GUMBO

Great big gawky Gumbo Cole
Couldn't stop growing to save his soul.
Gave up eating, gave up drink,
Sat in the closet, hoped to shrink;
But he grew and grew till he burst the door,
His head went through to the upper floor,
His feet reached down to the cellar door.
He grew still more till the house came down
And Gumbo Cole stepped out on the town
And smashed it in like an old anthill!
Never stopped growing, never will.
Ten times as tall as a telephone pole,
Too big for his breeches—Gumbo Cole!

# BANJO TUNE

Plunk -a- Plunk! Plunk -a- Plunk!
I sit in the attic on an old trunk.

Plunk -a- Plunk!

Locked in the old trunk is my wife,
And she may be there for the rest of her life.

Plunk -a- Plunk!

She screams, "Let me out of here, you fool!"
I say, "I will when your soup gets cool."

Plunk -a- Plunk!

She screams, "Let me out or I'll bean you, brother!"
I say, "Now, come on, tell me another!"

Plunk -a- Plunk!

To keep one's wife in a trunk is wrong,
But I keep mine there for the sake of my song.

Plunk -a- Plunk!

My song is hokum, my song is bunk,
And there's just a wad of old clothes in this trunk;
Not even the junkman would want this junk!

Plunk -a- Plunk!

Plunk -a- Plunk!

Plunk!

# THE CROSSING OF
# MARY OF SCOTLAND

Mary, Mary, Queen of Scots,
Dressed in yellow polka dots,
Sailed one rainy winter day,
Sailed from Dover to Calais,
Sailed in tears, heart tied in knots;
Face broke out in scarlet spots
The size of yellow polka dots—
Forgot to take her *booster* shots,
Queen of Scotland, Queen of Scots!

# THE BLACK WIDOW
## *A Cautionary Tale*

A soldier, lately assigned a billet,*
Saw a black widow spider and set out to kill it;
But he tripped while clutching a sizzling skillet.
Flame shot up, destroying the billet,
And overcooking the eggs in the skillet.

*Moral*
To kill a black widow won't always help, will it?

* *Billet:* lodging or quarters for a soldier.

# BAD BOY'S SWAN SONG

*The evening waddles over the fields like a turkey.*
        —James Reaney

The evening waddles over the fields like a turkey,
 And I, for one, have really cooked my goose—
I who started the day out fresh and perky,
 Feeling on top of the world, all fast and loose.

I took apart my sister's pretty wagon
 And stuffed the parts (by mistake) down the laundry chute,
Then wrapped the box back up, put ribbon and tag on,
 So when she opens it up, she'll scream, "You brute!"

When Father returns in a little while from work, he
 Will surely blow his top—just my bad luck.
Evening waddles over the fields like a turkey;
 And I'm a gone gosling, yes, sir, a real dead duck.

# THE ANTIMACASSAR
# AND THE OTTOMAN

"I am leaving this house as soon as I can,"
Said the Antimacassar to the Ottoman.
"I hate this room, I loathe this chair,
I can't stand people's oily hair,
I long for a breath of mountain air.
    I will fly away to Turkistan;
    Will you come with me, dear Ottoman?"

The Ottoman sighed and said: "Oh, man!
I will certainly go with you if I can.
I, too, am sick of this overstuffed chair
And want nothing more than a breath of air!
I'm weary of having my praises sung
By an ugly pot of Mother-in-law's tongue!
Give me a mountain's twisted shapes
For the arsenic green of those green drapes;
Give me the green of a foreign land
For the green of that green umbrella stand!
I daily see a dreadful menace
In that awful painted scene of Venice
That glows at night like dead desire
Above an artificial fire.
I know by heart the sad tweet-tweets
Of those pale sky-blue parakeets!
And all I can hear is a high-pitched snicker
From that chaise longue of painted wicker!
The African violets are wet,
They haven't dried their pink eyes yet;
Day after day their hot tears come
Across the cold linoleum!
They *loathe* this room as much as I!
    Tears, idle tears! *I* cannot cry.
    Do let us go—do let us fly!"


But an Ottoman, it cannot fly,
And an Antimacassar—who knows why?—
Is pinned in permanence to a chair.
So when morning came, they both were there;
And no window opened to let in the air,
    And neither had flown to Turkistan—
    The Antimacassar nor the Ottoman.

# FLIGHT OF
# THE ONE-EYED BAT

The night has a thousand eyes,
    The one-eyed bat but one,
Which it opens as it flies
    Straight at the setting sun.

Straight at the sun it flies,
    The sun that slowly sinks;
Night blinks its thousand eyes,
    The bat's eye never blinks

But enlarges while it flies
    And jerks its webbed black wings
Like the ribs of an old umbrella
    Or the coils of old bedsprings;

Flies over rooftops and chimneys,
    Over graveyards and hotels,
While factories blow their whistles
    And churches toll their bells;

Flies till the spotlight's extinguished,
    A ruby curtain rung down,
Till the town has clutched at the country,
    And the country swallowed the town;

Flies till the moon's on a clothespin,
    Till the Milky Way dangles from wire,
Till the cat creeps out of the coal bin,
    And the kettle sings by the fire;

Flies till its mission's accomplished,
  A head-on dark deed done:
Night opens a thousand eyes,
  The bat closes one.

# FLIGHT OF
# THE LONG-HAIRED YAK

One Tuesday night the long-haired Yak
Flew up to the Moon with a thunder crack;
 He spent next day
 At the Milky Way,
And paid for his room with the coat off his back.

He walked on the floor and it went Crick-Crack
And a board flew up and hit him, Whack!
 And down he fell
 In an ink-black well,
And bent his knees and broke his back.

They carted him off to a tarpapered shack
And sent for pills from Dr. Quack,
 But that was the end
 Of our long-haired friend;
So they covered him up with a gunnysack.

The mourners came in robes of black
And said: "He's dead. Alas! Alack!
 He died too soon,
 He flew to the Moon
Last Tuesday night, and came right back!"

The Moral is: Remove your pack,
And hang your cocked hat on the rack.
 You may long to stray
 Toward the Milky Way,
But you'd better keep to the beaten track.

When your heart goes Thump! and things go black
Like thick smoke belching from a stack,
And the fat flies buzz, and the lean beaks clack,
And the Bloody Blue-nosed Bores attack,

Buzz! Buzz! Buzz!

Clack! Clack! Clack!

Yickety Yak!   Yak! Yak! Yak!

Poor Yorick-Yak!

*You had better keep to the beaten track!*
*You had better keep to the beaten track!*

# BALLAD OF
# BLACK AND WHITE

When once I walked out for a breath of fresh air,
I looked up and saw a fat Polar Bear,
    Who was eating ice cream
    By a cold Arctic stream
While the barber, a Penguin, trimmed his white hair,
       While a Penguin trimmed his white hair.

"Will you tell me," I said to the Bear by the stream,
"Why things as they are are not as they seem?
    Will you tell me," I said,
    "Why the sky that looks red,
In point of fact, is as white as that cream,
       In fact, *is* as white as that cream?"

"I will tell you, my friend," said the fat Polar Bear
While the Penguin continued to trim his white hair,
    "Things are not as they seem;
    If they were as they seem,
Then how, my good friend, could they be as they are,
       Then how could they be as they are?

"How, may I ask, could the ice in that stream
Which one might mistake for vanilla ice cream,
    Strawberry, peach,
    Just out of reach,
Be anything else but the ice in that stream,
       Be else but the ice in that stream?"

"How could it indeed," I said to the Bear,
"Be other than ice in this Eskimo air?
        Or so it would seem
        To one in a dream,
Or rather to one in a simple nightmare,
            To one in a simple nightmare!"

The strange Polar Bear, his dark eye agleam,
Then bade me farewell with the greatest esteem;
        I awoke in the night,
        And black was as white,
And chocolate was as vanilla ice cream,
            Chocolate, vanilla ice cream.

# MAY-AS-WELL

In the Citadel of May-as-Well
On the banks of the bonny Quite,
The armies march from right to left,
And then from left to right.

To get wherever they are going
These enterprising men
All go the way the wind is blowing,
Then back with it again.

From A to B they come and go,
From B to A to B,
And so keep everything so-so,
And all so easily.

The ranks rebel in Ne'er-Do-Well,
The workmen quit in Spite,
But all is well in May-as-Well,
All Quiet on the Quite.

# THE TYPEWRITER BIRD

The Typewriter Bird with the pitchfork beak
Will sing when its feathers are given a tweak,
Will sing from now till the end of the week
In the typewritten language that typewriters speak,
                    The Typewriter Bird.

Ugly and clickety, cheerful and gay,
Skyscraper-blue or tenement-gray,
It hops up and down in its rotary way
And sings till the bell rings, Hip Hooray!
                    The Typewriter Bird.

The Typewriter Bird with the spotted fan
Flies off to the jungles of Yucatán,
Where perched on a table of old rattan,
It sings like water that drips in a pan,
                    The Typewriter Bird.

It sings like water Drip-Drop! Drip-Drop!
That falls on a corrugated-iron rooftop,
In a round tin pan on the wobbly rattan—
Drip-Drop! Jim-Jim! Drip-Drop! Drip-Drop!
                    The Typewriter Bird.

The Typewriter Bird is a terrible bore;
It sings—Jim-Jim!—and it sings encore.
It sings in London and Singapore;
It flies to the ceiling, it drops to the floor,
It bangs on the wall, it knocks at the door,
But thrown out the window, it sings no more,
                    The Typewriter Bird.

# MR. SMITH

How rewarding to know Mr. Smith,
  Whose writings at random appear!
Some think him a joy to be with
  While others do not, it is clear.

His eyes are somewhat Oriental,
  His fingers are notably long;
His disposition is gentle,
  He will jump at the sound of a gong.

His chin is quite smooth and uncleft,
  His face is clean-shaven and bright,
His right arm looks much like his left,
  His left leg, it goes with his right.

He has friends in the arts and the sciences;
  He knows only one talent scout;
He can cope with most kitchen appliances,
  But in general prefers dining out.

When young he collected matchboxes,
  He now collects notebooks and hats;
He has eaten *roussettes* (flying foxes),
  Which are really the next thing to bats!

He has never set foot on Majorca,
  He has been to Tahiti twice
But will seldom, no veteran walker,
  Take two steps when one will suffice.

He abhors motorbikes and boiled cabbage;
    Zippers he just tolerates;
He is wholly indifferent to cribbage,
    And cuts a poor figure on skates.

He weeps by the side of the ocean,
    And goes back the way that he came;
He calls out his name with emotion—
    It returns to him always the same.

It returns on the wind and he hears it
    While the waves make a rustle around;
The dark settles down, and he fears it.
    He fears its thin, crickety sound.

He thinks more and more as time passes,
    Rarely opens a volume on myth.
Until mourned by the tall prairie grasses,
    How rewarding to know Mr. Smith!

# THE KING OF SPAIN

*"I like this book,"* said the King of Spain.
*"I think I'll read it through again."*